HUMILITY

The Great Virtue

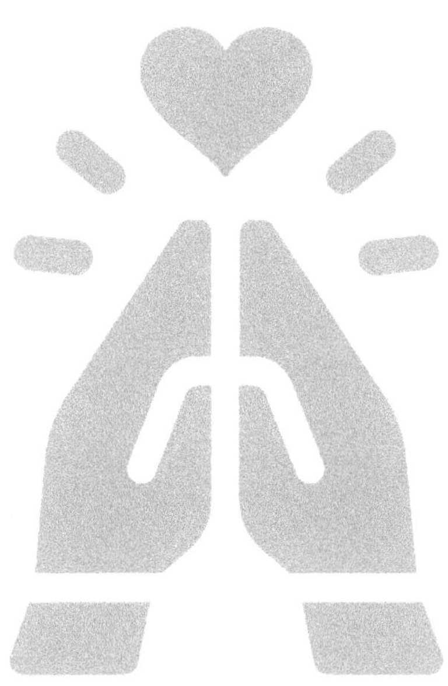

BY

BEBUH DIVINE

2 Chronicles 7:14 King James Version (Kjv)

If My People, Which Are Called By My Name, Shall Humble Themselves, And Pray, And Seek My Face, And Turn From Their Wicked Ways; Then Will I Hear From Heaven, And Will Forgive Their Sin, And Will Heal Their Land.

ACKNOWLEDGEMENTS

I will like to acknowledge,

Jesus Christ the saviour of my soul,my love and my God for his inspiration and tender care He offers me daily. Without Him, this work will not have been possible.

I want to offer special thanks to my family for their support and critique.

I would like to acknowledge materials that helped me accomplish this work.

1 The Holy bible (KJV, GNT, NIV)

2 Humility the journey towards holiness by Andrew Murray

TABLE OF CONTENTS

INTRODUCTION

"HUMILITY" The Great Virtue

is a book aimed at helping the children of God to rediscover the blessings God has reserved for the humble. It is also helps the children of God to cultivate the virtue of humility. This book outlines the lucrative and indescribable benefits of humility. The book also outlines the high level of importance this virtue has in the eyes of God.

CHAPTER 01

WHAT IS HUMILITY?

It is the virtue of having a modest or low view of one's importance.

It is firstly acknowledging our nothingness before God.

Humility is submitting our souls to God.

Humility is Making God our all.

Humility is Submitting our lives to God's commandments.

Humility is asking and following God's opinion on any subject.

Humility is Refusing to question God's wisdom.

Humility is living in obedience to God's laws at the expense of circular knowledge.

Humility is seeing ourselves as people of equal dignity, not superior to other humans.

Humility is emptying oneself so that God can take the lead.

Humility is allowing God to rule one's heart.

It is not about bowing to greet everyone we see; that's eye service. Humility is a deeper virtue born from the spirit of God and present in man's heart.

Humility is acknowledging our nothingness without God and our constant need for God at every moment.

Humility is also an acknowledgment of others and the importance of their contributions to our lives. No one can succeed alone.

Everyone is a solution to a problem. We all have strengths and weaknesses and need each other to succeed. Acknowledging this from the heart is humility.

Humility is acknowledging that we are not perfect and are fallible. When we fall, asking for forgiveness from God and man is humility.

A proud person justifies his mistakes and tries to legalise his flaws.

The first man, Adam, justified himself and blamed the woman and God for his disobedience.

Eve blamed the snake for her disobedience.

None of them humbled themselves, accepted their mistake before God, and asked for pardon. As a result, their punishment was severe. They were cast out of the Garden of Eden.

Blaming others for your mistake is a sign of pride.

CHAPTER 02

WAYS TO CULTIVATE HUMILITY

1. Prioritise God's word over circular wisdom

Luke 6.46

Why do you call me lord lord and yet not do the things I tell you?

Peter had circular wisdom for fishing; as an experienced fisherman, he toiled all night and caught nothing. He knew the night was the best time for fishing as the fish would not see the net.

Also, fishing near the seashore was not the best place to cast the net, yet he submitted his circular knowledge to God's wisdom.

And said "At your word I will cast the net."

So, he caught a great number of fish at God's word.

Luke 5:4-10

When he had finished speaking, he said to Simon, "Put out into deep water, and let down the nets for a catch."

5 Simon answered, "Master, we've worked hard all night and haven't caught anything. But because you say so, I will let down the nets."

6 When they had done so, they caught such a large number of fish that their nets began to break.

7 So they signalled their partners in the other boat to come and help them, and they came and filled both boats so full that they began to sink.

8 When Simon Peter saw this, he fell at Jesus' knees and said, "Go away from me, Lord; I am a sinful man!"

9 For he and all his companions were astonished at the catch of fish they had taken,

10 and so were James and John, the sons of Zebedee, Simon's partners.

11 Then Jesus said to Simon, "Don't be afraid; from now on you will fish for people."

Humility is shown by obeying God's word even though it contradicts personal thoughts and circular knowledge.

2. Do Jobs below your status

Jesus is the son of God; still, He humbled himself to become man, accepted the worst treatment reserved for thieves, and was despised to the point that Barabbas, a murderer and robber, was preferred over Him. He accepted crucifixion just to save mankind. Heaven was His status, yet He lowered Himself to the earth; we must follow His example.

Philippians 2.5-9

In your relationships with one another, have the same mindset as Christ Jesus:

6 Who, being in very nature[a] God,

   did not consider equality with God something to be used to his own advantage;

7 rather, he made himself nothing by taking the very nature[b] of a servant, being made in human likeness.

8 And being found in appearance as a man, he humbled himself by becoming obedient to death— even death on a cross!

9 Therefore God exalted him to the highest place and gave him the name that is above every name,

3. Serve People with Love

Jesus says, "I am among you as he who serves."

Luke 22:27

Humility is cultivated by service to our fellow brothers and sisters with love. Jesus was not arrogant; He served people irrespective of their social class.

4. Serve Those Entrusted to Your Care

Jesus washed His disciples' feet and taught them to do the same. In the world, it is the servant who washes his master's feet, but in the kingdom, the greatest are called to be servants and slaves to all.

Mathew 20.25-26

Jesus called them together and said, "You know that the rulers of the Gentiles lord it over them, and their high officials exercise authority over them. 26 Not so with you. Instead, whoever wants to become great among you must be your servant, 27 and whoever wants to be first must be your slave.

We are called as Christians to wash the feet of our fellow brothers and sisters, to serve them with humility, overlook offences, and forgive mistakes.

CHAPTER 03

GOD CHERISHES HUMILITY SO MUCH

The first teaching of Jesus was about humility in the sermon on the Mount **(Mathew 5:3).**

The very first words of Jesus were humility.

It was so important to Jesus that He preached on it first, giving it this great virtue, unique, and primordial importance.

Mathew 5:3, says, "Blessed are the poor in spirit the kingdom of God belongs to them.

A poor spirit is a humble spirit. God promises the inheritance of Heaven to the humble.

Jesus did not stop there. He also promised the inheritance of the earth to the humble.

Matthew 5.5 says, "Blessed are the **humble**, they shall inherit the earth."

Humility is so great in the eyes of God that He has willed both the heavens and the earth to the humble. Every child of God must strive to cultivate a humble character because God has placed the greatest value on this virtue called humility.

He has willed all His riches in heaven and on earth to the possessors of this powerful virtue called humility.

Clothe Yourself with Humility

God wants us to clothe ourselves with virtues, especially humility, instead of looking for the best designer clothes, which are mere smoke in the eyes of Christ.

Therefore, clothe yourself with humility.

"Here, there is no Gentile or Jew, circumcised or uncircumcised, barbarian, Scythian, slave or free, but Christ is all, and is in all. Therefore, as God's chosen people, holy and dearly loved, clothe yourselves with compassion, kindness, humility, gentleness and patience." (Colossians 3:11-12)

Humility is Equal to Faith

Humility is directly proportional to faith; the more humble you are, the more faith you have.

A good example is the healing of the centurion servant.

The Faith of the Centurion (Luke 7:1-10)

The centurion was a man who possessed great humility and found himself unworthy to receive Jesus in his home. As a result, Jesus equated his humility to faith. Jesus said, "I have not found such great faith in Israel."

Luke 7:1-10

When Jesus had finished saying all this to the people who were listening, he entered Capernaum. 2 There a centurion's servant, whom his master valued highly, was sick and about to die. 3 The centurion heard of Jesus and sent some elders of the Jews to him, asking him to come and heal his servant. 4 When they came to Jesus, they pleaded earnestly with him, "This man deserves to have you do this, 5 because he loves our nation and has built our synagogue." 6 So Jesus went with them.

He was not far from the house when the centurion sent friends to say to him: "Lord, don't trouble yourself, for I do not deserve to have you come under my roof. 7 That is why I did not even consider myself worthy to come to you. But say the word, and my servant will be healed. 8 For I myself am a man under authority, with soldiers under me. I tell this one, 'Go,' and he goes; and that one, 'Come,' and he comes. I say to my servant, 'Do this,' and he does it."

9 When Jesus heard this, he was amazed at him, and turning to the crowd following him, he said, "I tell you, I have not found such great faith even in Israel." 10 Then the men who had been sent returned to the house and found the servant well.

The centurion, full of humility, did not see himself as worthy of hosting Jesus. The Lord Jesus equated the centurion's humility to faith in God.

The Faith of a Canaanite Woman

(Matthew 15:21-28)

Another example is the healing of the Canaanite woman's daughter.

Jesus tested her humility by telling her it was not right to give the children's bread to dogs.

She had the choice to be offended and go her way for being referred to as a dog. She understood it was a test of humility and answered, "Even dogs eat crumbs from their master's table, and Jesus praised her faith and healed her daughter.

21 Leaving that place, Jesus withdrew to the region of Tyre and Sidon.

22 A Canaanite woman from that vicinity came to him, crying out, "Lord, Son of David, have mercy on me! My daughter is demon-possessed and suffering terribly."

23 Jesus did not answer a word. So, his disciples came to him and urged him, "Send her away, for she keeps crying out after us."

24 He answered, "I was sent only to the lost sheep of Israel."

25 The woman came and knelt before him. "Lord, help me!" she said.

26 He replied, "It is not right to take the children's bread and toss it to the dogs."

27 "Yes, it is, Lord," she said. "Even the dogs eat the crumbs that fall from their master's table."

28 Then Jesus said to her, "Woman, you have great faith! Your request is granted." And her daughter was healed at that moment.

The woman humbled herself and refused to get angry, and when Jesus saw her great humility, He equated it to great faith.

CHAPTER 04

THE BLESSINGS OF HUMILITY

1. Inheritance Of The Kingdom Of Heaven

"Blessed are the poor in spirit, for theirs is the kingdom of God." (Matthew 5.3)

Poverty of spirit is a humble spirit. God has reserved the kingdom of heaven for the humble.

2. Inheritance Of The Earth

"Blessed are the humble for they shall inherit the earth." (Matthew 5:5)

God who created the earth has willed His creation to the humble; therefore, every child of God must make deliberate efforts to grow in humility in order to inherit the earth.

3. An Unusually Close Relationship With God

Moses was the humblest man in the world in his time. As a result, God spoke to him face to face. He was a spirit-filled prophet who interacted with divinity. God entrusted to him the story of creation.

Numbers 12:3

"Now the man Moses was very meek, **(humble)**above all the men which were upon the face of the earth."

"And there arose not a prophet since in Israel like unto Moses, whom the Lord knew face to face." **(Deuteronomy 34:10)**

The humility of Moses cleared the way for an unusually close relationship with God.

God Himself testified of the special relationship he had with moses. His Humility made God to relate with him in a special way . when other prophets tried to equate themselves to moses God intervened to put them back in their place.

Numbers 12:1-15.
Miriam and Aaron Oppose Moses

12 Miriam and Aaron spoke against Moses because of the Cushite woman whom he had married, for he had married a Cushite woman.

2 And they said, "Has the LORD indeed spoken only through Moses? Has he not spoken through us also?" And the LORD heard it.

3 Now the man Moses was very meek, more than all people who were on the face of the earth.

4 And suddenly the LORD said to Moses and to Aaron and Miriam, "Come out, you three, to the tent of meeting." And the three of them came out.

5 And the LORD came down in a pillar of cloud and stood at the entrance of the tent and called Aaron and Miriam, and they both came forward.

6 And he said, "Hear my words: If there is a prophet among you, I the LORD make myself known to him in a vision; I speak with him in a dream.

7 Not so with my servant Moses. He is faithful in all my house.

8 With him I speak mouth to mouth, clearly, and not in riddles, and he beholds the form of the LORD. Why then were you not afraid to speak against my servant Moses?"

9 And the anger of the LORD was kindled against them, and he departed.

10 When the cloud removed from over the tent, behold, Miriam was leprous, like snow. And Aaron turned toward Miriam, and behold, she was leprous.

11 And Aaron said to Moses, "Oh, my lord, do not punish us because we have done foolishly and have sinned.

12 Let her not be as one dead, whose flesh is half eaten away when he comes out of his mother's womb."

13 And Moses cried to the LORD, "O God, please heal her—please."

14 But the LORD said to Moses, "If her father had but spit in her face, should she not be shamed seven days? Let her be shut outside the camp seven days, and after that she may be brought in again."

15 So Miriam was shut outside the camp seven days, and the people did not set out on the march till Miriam was brought in again.

Greatness

"Whoever makes himself great will be humbled, and whoever humbles himself will be made great." **(Matthew 23:12)**

Moses was very meek, and God made him very great in the land of Egypt.

"Now the man Moses was very meek, above all the men which were upon the face of the earth." **(Numbers 12:3)**

"And the Lord gave the people favour in the sight of the Egyptians. Moreover, the man Moses was very great in the land of Egypt, in the sight of Pharaoh's servants and in the sight of the people." **(Exodus 11:3)**

The humility of Moses attracted God, and for that reason, God made him very great.

God has promised to exalt all those who humble themself **(Matthew 23:12).**

So, the way to greatness is humility.

4. Forgiveness

God almighty has promised to forgive those who humble themselves before Him.

"If My people who are called by My name will **humble** themselves, and pray and seek My face, and turn from their wicked ways, then I will hear from heaven, and will forgive their sin and heal their land." **(2 Chronicles 7:14)**

5. The Grace Of God

God resists the proud and shows grace to the **humble**.

"God opposes the proud but gives grace to the humble." **(James 4:6.)**

If you want God's favour or grace, you must be humble. That is the eligibility requirement we must meet.

6. Healing

God has promised to heal the humble.

2 Chronicles 7:14 (KJV)

"If my people, which are called by my name, shall humble themselves, and pray, and seek my face, and turn from their wicked ways; then will I hear from heaven, and will forgive their sin, and will heal their land."

The first requirement for the healing of the land is humility.

As children of God, we must learn to humble ourselves before God if we want to see God's healing grace.

Another example of a man whose humility moved God to heal him is the leper in the Gospel of Matthew.

Matthew 8:2-3

A man with leprosy came and knelt before him and said, "Lord, if you are willing, you can make me clean."

Jesus reached out his hand and touched the man. "I am willing," he said. "Be clean!" Immediately he was cleansed of his leprosy.

He humbled himself and knelt before Jesus and asked for Healing Grace, and Jesus healed him.

7. Restoration Of Lost Glory

King Manasseh had led Israel away from God by practising all kinds of evil; idol worship, child sacrifice, sorcery, etc. God warned him, but he paid no attention, so God brought a foreign Army to arrest him and keep him in jail. In his trouble and misfortune, He humbled himself before God and prayed, and God had mercy and restored him to kinghood. His humility led to the restoration of his lost glory.

Manasseh, King of Judah

33 Manasseh was twelve years old when he became king, and he reigned in Jerusalem fifty-five years.

2 He did evil in the eyes of the Lord, following the detestable practices of the nations the Lord had driven out before the Israelites.

3 He rebuilt the high places his father Hezekiah had demolished; he also erected altars to the Baals and made Asherah poles. He bowed down to all the starry hosts and worshipped them.

4 He built altars in the temple of the Lord, of which the Lord had said, "My Name will remain in Jerusalem forever."

5 In both courts of the temple of the Lord, he built altars to all the starry hosts.

6 He sacrificed his children in the fire in the Valley of Ben Hinnom, practised divination and witchcraft, sought omens, and consulted mediums and spiritists. He did much evil in the eyes of the Lord, arousing his anger.

7 He took the image he had made and put it in God's temple, of which God had said to David and to his son Solomon, "In this temple and in Jerusalem, which I have chosen out of all the tribes of Israel, I will put my Name forever.

8 I will not again make the feet of the Israelites leave the land I assigned to your ancestors, if only they will be careful to do everything I commanded them concerning all the laws, decrees and regulations given through Moses."

9 But Manasseh led Judah and the people of Jerusalem astray, so that they did more evil than the nations the Lord had destroyed before the Israelites.

10 The Lord spoke to Manasseh and his people, but they paid no attention.

11 So the Lord brought against them the army commanders of the king of Assyria, who took Manasseh prisoner, put a hook in his nose, bound him with bronze shackles and took him to Babylon.

12 In his distress he sought the favour of the Lord his God and **humbled himself greatly before the God of his ancestors**.

13 And when he prayed to him, the Lord was moved by his entreaty and listened to his plea; so, he brought him back to Jerusalem and to his kingdom. Then Manasseh knew that the Lord is God.

14 Afterward he rebuilt the outer wall of the City of David, west of the Gihon spring in the valley, as far as the entrance of the Fish Gate and encircling the hill of Ophel; he also made it much higher. He stationed military commanders in all the fortified cities in Judah.

15 He got rid of the foreign gods and removed the image from the temple of the Lord, as well as all the altars he had built on the temple hill and in Jerusalem; and he threw them out of the city.

16 Then he restored the altar of the Lord and sacrificed fellowship offerings and thank offerings on it, and told Judah to serve the Lord, the God of Israel.

17 The people, however, continued to sacrifice at the high places, but only to the Lord their God.

18 The other events of Manasseh's reign, including his prayer to his God and the words the seers spoke to him in the name of the Lord, the God of Israel, are written in the annals of the kings of Israel.[a]

19 His prayer and how God was moved by his entreaty, as well as all his sins and unfaithfulness, and the sites where he built high places and set up Asherah poles and idols before he humbled himself—all these are written in the records of the seers.[b]

20 Manasseh rested with his ancestors and was buried in his palace. And Amon his son succeeded him as king.

Humility before God has the power to restore your lost glory

8. *Humility Bring God's Guidance*

God guides the humble. What a blessing to have God as your guide and your teacher. If you want such a precious blessing, you must pay a little price called humility.

Psalms 25.9

He guides the **humble** in what is right

  and teaches them his way.

May God be our guide. Oh God, help us to humble ourselves so that you can be our guide and teacher.

9. *HUMILITY Attracts God´S WISDOM*

"When pride comes, then comes disgrace, but with humility comes wisdom." (PROVERBS 11:2)

The Bible tells us pride does not walk alone; if you allow it into your heart, it comes with disgrace.   Also, humility does not walk alone; it comes with wisdom. If you welcome humility into your heart, you are welcoming wisdom.

10.   *Humility Brings The Fear Of The Lord*

PROVERBS 22:4 "Humility is the fear of the Lord; its wages are riches and honour and life."

God tells us in Proverbs 22:4 that to prove our reverence to Him, we must be humble, and the reward is greatness, riches, honour, and life.

May God help us cultivate this precious virtue so we can benefit from these lucrative rewards.

11.   *Humility Brings Honour*

Proverbs 18:12

Before destruction the heart of a man is haughty, And before honour is humility.

The way to honour is humility; if you want to be honoured by God, practice humility.

CHAPTER 05

THE DESTRUCTIVE AND DAMAGING POTENTIAL OF PRIDE

1. God Resists the proud.

"Therefore, it says, "God opposes the proud but gives grace to the humble." (James 4.6)

If God is opposing you, your life will be hell on earth. Pride makes God your enemy, so failure is sure to come upon you.

2. Humiliation and disgrace

And whosoever shall exalt himself shall be abased, and he that shall humble himself shall be exalted. (Matthew 23:12)

God has promised to disgrace and humiliate the proud like Satan. If you want equality with God, you will be humiliated, disgraced, and cursed for eternity.

3. Pride Brings God's Punishment of Sickness

Uzziah, who had earlier been faithful to God, became proud and arrogant and offered a sacrifice reserved for priests. His action provoked God to anger, and God struck him with disease.

He was unclean for the rest of his days.

Uzziah's Pride and Punishment.

2 chronicles 26:16-19

16 But when he was strong, he grew **proud**, **to his destruction**. For he was unfaithful to the Lord his God and entered the temple of the Lord to burn incense on the altar of incense. 17 But Azariah the priest went in after him, with eighty priests of the Lord who were men of valor, 18 and they withstood King Uzziah and said to him, "It is not for you, Uzziah, to burn incense to the Lord, but for the priests, the sons of Aaron, who are consecrated to burn incense. Go out of the sanctuary, for you have done wrong, and it will bring you no honour from the Lord God." 19 Then Uzziah was angry. Now he had a censer in his hand to burn incense, and when he became angry with the priests, leprosy[a] broke out on his forehead in the presence of the priests in the house of the Lord, by the altar of incense. 20 And Azariah the chief priest and all the priests looked at him, and behold, he was leprous in his forehead! And they rushed him out quickly, and he himself hurried to go out, because the Lord had struck him.

Uzziah had the last opportunity to humble himself before God when the Priests pointed out his wrong, but he didn't. Instead, in pride, he resorted to anger, and God struck him with leprosy. No matter how high you are, your virtues are higher than you.

4. Pride Brings God's Punishment of Captivity

Therefore, I'm bringing the worst of the nations, who will take possession of their houses. I'll cause the pride of the mighty to cease, and their sanctuaries will be profaned. (EZEKIEL 7:24)

The people in Ezekiel's time allowed pride to possess them, so God punished them by dispossessing their land and possessions, which made them proud. Pride will only bring disgrace to one's life.

5. Pride brings God's Punishment of Dethronement

Nebuchadnezzar was proud and claimed he built his temple by his might, and God dethroned him and made him eat grass for seven years in the wilderness.

Daniel Interprets the Second Dream-- Daniel 4:19-33

19 Then Daniel, whose name was Belteshazzar, was dismayed for a while, and his thoughts alarmed him. The king answered and said, "Belteshazzar, let not the dream or the interpretation alarm you." Belteshazzar answered and said, "My lord, may the dream be for those who hate you and its interpretation for your enemies! **20** The tree you saw, which grew and became strong, so that its top reached to heaven, and it was visible to the end of the whole earth, **21** whose leaves were beautiful and its fruit abundant, and in which was food for all, under which beasts of the field found shade, and in whose branches the birds of the heavens lived— **22** it is you, O king, who have grown and become strong. Your greatness has grown and reaches to heaven, and your dominion to the ends of the earth. **23** And because the king saw a watcher, a holy one, coming down from heaven and saying, 'Chop down the tree and destroy it, but leave the stump of its roots in the earth, bound with a band of iron and bronze, in the tender grass of the field, and let him be wet with the dew of heaven, and let his portion be with the beasts of the field, till seven periods of time pass over him,' **24** this is the interpretation, O king: It is a decree of the Most High, which has come upon my lord the king, **25** that you shall be driven from among men, and your dwelling shall be with the beasts of the field. You shall be made to eat grass like an ox, and you shall be wet with the dew of heaven, and seven periods of time shall pass over you, till you know that the Most High rules the kingdom of men and gives it to whom he will. **26** And as it was commanded to leave the stump of the roots of the tree, your kingdom shall be confirmed for you from the time that you know that Heaven rules. **27** Therefore, O king, let my counsel be acceptable to you: break off your sins by practising righteousness, and your iniquities by showing mercy to the oppressed, that there may perhaps be a lengthening of your prosperity."

Nebuchadnezzar's Humiliation

28 All this came upon King Nebuchadnezzar. **29** At the end of twelve months he was walking on the roof of the royal palace of Babylon, **30** and the king answered and said, "Is not this great Babylon, which I have built by my mighty power as a royal residence and for the glory of my majesty?" **31** While the words were still in the king's mouth, there fell a voice from heaven, "O King Nebuchadnezzar, to you it is spoken: The kingdom has departed from you, **32** and you shall be driven from among men, and your dwelling shall be with the beasts of the field. And you shall be made to eat grass like an ox, and seven periods of time shall pass over you, until you know that the Most High rules the kingdom of men and gives it to whom he will." **33** Immediately the word was fulfilled against Nebuchadnezzar. He was driven from among men and ate grass like an ox, and his body was wet with the dew of heaven till his hair grew as long as eagles' feathers, and his nails were like birds' claws.

Humility can preserve and maintain God's blessing, but pride will lead to the fall of any man, no matter how highly placed he is.

6. Pride Brings God's Punishment of Death

God's angel struck Herod to be eaten by worms.

Herod was a man who allowed the vice of pride to consume him. He made a high throne for himself and sat, receiving praise from people who said he was a god. He did not humble himself and paid for his pride with a disgraceful death of being eaten by worms.   Beware of pride.

Acts 12:20-23

The Death of Herod

20 Now Herod was angry with the people of Tyre and Sidon, and they came to him with one accord, and having persuaded Blastus, the king's chamberlain, [b] they asked for peace, because their country depended on the king's country for food. 21 On an appointed day Herod put on his royal robes, took his seat upon the throne, and delivered an oration to them. 22 And the people were shouting, "The voice of a god, and not of a man!" 23 Immediately an angel of the Lord struck him down, because he did not give God the glory, and he was eaten by worms and breathed his last.

7. God Hates a Proud Heart

The LORD detests all the proud of heart. Be sure of this: They will not go unpunished. **Proverbs 16:5**

God has promised not to allow anyone with pride in his heart to go unpunished.

Everyone who wants to escape God's wrath must give up pride and embrace true humility of heart.

God does not only punish proud individuals; He pushes proud cities, nations, and the world at large.

An example is Jeremiah 50:31-32. God proclaimed punishment to the most glorious city at the time, Babylon.

Jeremiah 50:31 Behold, I am against you, O you most proud, says the Lord GOD of hosts: for your day has come, the time that I will punish you. The arrogant one shall stumble and fall, with no one to raise him up and I will kindle a fire in his cities,

and it will devour everything around him.

Today, Babylon is in ruins and uninhabited to testify to God's sovereignty over the world.

Satan is your father and king if you have pride in yourself.

he is a king over all the children of pride.

Job 41:34

CHAPTER 06

JESUS WANTS YOU TO BE HUMBLE

Learn from me, for I am gentle and humble in spirit.

"Take my yoke and put it on you, and learn from me, because I am gentle and humble in spirit; and you will find rest." **Matthew 11:29**

Jesus tells us that His heart is full of humility, and His followers cannot afford to embrace the evil of pride. The more humble you are, the closer you are to Christ.

Jesus instructs us in **Luke 14:8-14** to take the lowest seat when invited to the feast to prove our humility. The proud want the best place because they think they are more worthy than others; they see themselves above others.

In other words, we should guard ourselves from pride. Jesus asks us to take the lowest seats.

8 "When you are invited by anyone to a wedding feast, do not sit down in the best place, lest one more honorable than you be invited by him;

9 and he who invited you and him come and say to you, 'Give place to this man,' and then you begin with shame to take the lowest place.

10 But when you are invited, go and sit down in the lowest place, so that when he who invited you comes he may say to you, 'Friend, go up higher.' Then you will have glory in the presence of those who sit at the table with you.

11 For whoever exalts himself will be [a]humbled, and he who humbles himself will be exalted."

12 Then He also said to him who invited Him, "When you give a dinner or a supper, do not ask your friends, your brothers, your relatives, nor rich neighbors, lest they also invite you back, and you be repaid.

13 But when you give a feast, invite *the* poor, *the* [b]maimed, *the* lame, *the* blind.

14 And you will be blessed, because they cannot repay you; for you shall be repaid at the resurrection of the just."

JESUS Wants Complete Humility

Be completely humble and gentle.

Be completely humble and gentle; be patient, bearing with one another in love. Make every effort to keep the unity of the Spirit through the bond of peace. There is one body and one Spirit, just as you were called to one hope when you were called; one Lord, one faith, one baptism; one God and Father of all, who is over all and through all and in all. **Ephesians 4:2-6 NIV**

CONCLUSION

Jesus, our Lord, began his teaching ministry by teaching the importance of humility.

"Blessed are the poor in spirit for theirs is the kingdom of Heaven" **(a poor spirit is a humble spirit).** (Matthew 5:3 says)

"Blessed are the **humble** they shall inherit the earth." (Matthew 5:5)

Jesus has willed His creation, both the heavens and the earth, to the humble.

He values this virtue greatly, and so must we, His followers.

Prayer; Lord Jesus, help us to cultivate in our hearts the great and indispensable virtue of **HUMILITY.**

In Jesus' name Amen.

ABOUT THE AUTHOR

The Author "**Bebuh Divine**" is a seasoned evangelist with burning love for Christ . He is committed to the spread of the Gospel of Jesus Christ. He is a promoter of God's virtues such Humility , Purity, the love of God, honesty, Justice and Mercy and a Prayerful lifestyle.

www.ingramcontent.com/pod-product-compliance
Lightning Source LLC
Chambersburg PA
CBHW040206160726
48006CB00014B/1916